HAUNTED (

&

THEIR UNINVITED GUESTS

Martin Tapsell

Tivoli Publishing

68, Albert Road, DEAL CT14 9RB

First Published by Tivoli Publishing, 2016

Copyright   Martin Tapsell

Printed in Great Britain by BUSI-PRINT (Kent)
www.busi-print.co.uk
Tel 01304 613079

ISBN   978-0-9560954-2-8

Cover illustrations : The Empire, Leicester Square, London and on the back cover where the cashier jumped from in the Coronet, Nottinghill Gate. The photo on title page kindly permitted by Jamie Stam of Toronto

CONTENTS

INTRODUCTION

When visitors tour a live theatre, the question is often put – " is there a ghost?" Invariably , or so it seems, there is. I do not ask this question in a cinema, but was surprised how often staff told me of something paranormal. A cinema retains a powerful atmosphere after the film, but the guests who become attached to it, may return uninvited, whilst what was on the site before the cinema can be significant, not to mention any fatality during the cinema's construction.

The cases reported here are all in the public domain, so a cinema who finds a haunting not good for business need not suffer. A man who inadvertently bought an Erith cinema that was a morgue in WW2, found only children came in any numbers!! The author has not seen any ghosts himself, but knows people who have, so keeps an open mind. If people become spirits after death, but fail to move on to the Spirit World for personal reasons, ghost hunters will not resolve their problems, as they are out to prove the existence of ghosts, not rescue them. Most people will move on to the light quite soon, maybe staying on for their funeral, but those worried about their family, suddenly and violently deprived of life, or deeply attached to a building may linger on for decades – up to ten in cinemas!

If staff in a cinema see an apparition, or have something thrown at them or maybe have their shoulder tapped, the spirit is rarely evil, but just trying to share some unhappiness. Yet unlike in a private house, they are less likely to think the living have invaded their territory, but don't expect them to rush out before the credits or keep away during the night. They could be into films, as they were in life. People react in so many different ways to the supernatural – fear, embarrassment, ridicule, acceptance, (provided a presence is benign) or they may turn to clergy or mediums to have a quiet word. What you make of the paranormal is your business, but believers and unbelievers share a fascination

EAST ANGLIA

BEDFORD Be careful what you build on. The **Cineworld** is on the grounds of Newnham Priory, which may explain the sighting of a hooded monk-like figure in screen 4 and the toilets. Worse still the doors to screen 4 have opened violently by themselves and patrons hear scratching noises over their heads and even feel ghostly hands on their legs. Cold spots and strange unexplained sounds have been heard. One elderly cinemagoer recalled the cinema is on the site of a swimming pool, where the lockers would open by themselves and then bang shut at night. Is an usherette's nephew, who committed suicide by hanging from a tree in the park, partly responsible for ongoing phenomena?

IPSWICH The **Film Theatre** is inside the Town Hall. Several staff have reported a shadowy figure walking round the rear corridors near to the projection room, but identity unknown.

**Bedford
Cineworld**

CLACTON Peacocks stands on the site of the former **Kinema** (1913-62) where an unidentified suicide took place in the 1940s. That would explain the appearance of a man in a suit of that period, and maybe stamping feet sounds and doors opening and closing by themselves , if alas suicide failed to resolve the man's problems. Perhaps demolition helped.

KINGS LYNN   The **Majestic** has an unusual focus point – a clock tower dating from 1928. You Tube has a group of ghost hunters making their way up the tower – mainly an emergency staircase, from the ballroom or projection room. As often happens their equipment picked up sounds not made by the group, and worse one man gets separated from the rest when togetherness is needed for reassurance.

LUTON   The **Alma** cinema no longer exists, but here locals were forced out of their homes to make way for the cinema. Some put a curse on the Alma, although it lasted between 1929 and 1954. However, a construction worker fell to his death, and it's thought it was his ghostly presence that was seen subsequently. In multiplexes a particular screen can be affected, and in the modern **Cineworld**, from 2006 Screen 6 claimed for itself a mix of strange sounds, darting shadows and icy cold patches of air defying the central heating.

NORWICH   Controversy met a photograph taken in 2009 of a ghost seated in Cinema City. Mr Andrew Kitt was sure nobody had crossed his shot, and the cinema is certainly in an historic 14th century building. What period did the figure come from? – the photo is not clear enough to resolve this.

Home of the Ipswich Film Theatre

MIDLANDS

BELPER   Ritz. Usually it is animals who are most sensitive to the paranormal, but human beings can sense they are being watched. They may do in Belper where the original building held prisoners, who could be executed just for stealing food to keep their families alive. The current building began as the Town Hall and Law courts in 1882. Projectionist Roddy Buxton felt occasionally that he was being watched, and lighting in the rewind room went on and off of its own accord. Roddy left when the twin cinemas over the bingo hall closed in 1991, but since 2006 a single screen has operated, and we hope this was met with spirit approval! A weekly Thursday Silver Screen certainly has approval!

BIRMINGHAM   England's second city is not also second for the paranormal , and a cuttings file on ghosts in Birmingham library covered everything but cinemas!. It seems a cleaner working in what began in 1939 as the Danilo, Quinton (and is now the Reel) said the cinema was haunted in the 1980s. More specific, retired projectionist Raymond Mascord ,who worked at the **ABC**, Tyseley in the 1950s, was sure someone passed behind him as he sat by the projector. He made a search but found nobody, and knew one exit door led to a locked fire escape and the other to a switch room downstairs and the way out. But these were undisturbed so the mystery stayed with Raymond. In 1971 two witnesses saw a lady in green cross Victoria Road, but vanish . It was thought this might be a run over usherette from the Aston Cross Cinema.

ILKESTON   The **Scala** is old enough to have acquired a few   ghosts.   A   walled graveyard stood on the site before   1913.   A   cleaner unusually named Vambria Walters   often   told   her  husband Arthur she spotted figures walking round the cinema. One could be a member of the original cinema family, Mr Frank Hubert Brailsford, who was unhappy about some modernisation in the foyer area . A team of ghost hunters named Twilight Paranormal had a rewarding time with table tapping, ouija boards and recording sounds in 2014. The more modern **Ritz**, now a bingo hall, is not to be outdone, having apparitions of past owners and users, knockings, footsteps, sounds of doors opening and of cleaning. Clearly the investigators have more work to do. For more details visit hauntedilkeston.wix.com Are the Scala ghosts grade II listed with the cinema?

KETTERING Working in the 8 screen **Odeon** made a lady named Rachel nervous. There between 1997 and 2001, she soon heard the cinema was built on an ancient burial ground. Being susceptible to the occult, she felt nervous in auditoria on her own, imagining someone was watching her through the projection porthole. Some staff liked to play pranks to reinforce this fear, but screen 3 is the one to beware of. All this is confessed on mawgrim.co.uk and raises an interesting question – is it a more pleasant experience clearing up after a children's film than *The Exorcist?*

LEAMINGTON SPA The **Vue** is not a typical multiplex for the 6 screens occupy the former art deco **Regal** of 1931. In 2014, £500,000 was spent upgrading the facilities, hopefully to the approval of Edith Devis. She was the widow of an original benefactor of the town and funded the cinema herself, but she started appearing shortly after she died in a car crash.

LINCOLN   A rare case of we're watching them! The former **Radion** Cinema (1939-60) is now BBC Radio Lincolnshire. But as a cinema it had cold spots, a ghostly lady on the stage and even a phantom ice cream seller. The Radion was split up into floors for the BBC, who enterprisingly installed a ghost cam on the top floor in 2009, so any interested parties could monitor paranormal activity. But are they camera shy?

LONGTON   The Frank Matcham theatre was lost to fire in Jan, 1993, but a staff member fell from the later boarded off

top balcony, and was seen after bingo took root in 1966. So Mr Newman, the caretaker spotted a shadowy figure up there in 1971. Several days later the figure appeared again, and the caretaker's trained guard dog bristled with fear. A middle aged man was observed gliding between the seats but never found. R.I.P. to the **Empire.**

MANSFIELD

The metal cladding put on by **ABC** Cinemas in the 1960s hid the earlier origin of the Grand theatre, reconstructed in 1928. The cinema was tripled but closed in 1997 and Rileys

Snooker only used the ground floor screen, while the upper level decayed and pigeons and other occupants could make people jump. A church has now moved in, but Ghost Urbex has a video on You Tube, exploring the derelict areas which include the manager's flat. He, and an usher called Fred who died peacefully in a chair here are the most likely phantoms, but the video guide said she felt uneasy in certain areas, even that someone was pushing her up or downstairs. And after hearing a loud crash in one corner, then requesting to hear another, a second crash was provided as paranormal proof.

NEWCASTLE-UNDER-LYME   The Paranormal Database lists the haunting in the **Rex and Rio** plainly as "Woman" A staff member locking up in the late 1960s saw a woman heading for the toilets. He shouted to her to be quick, but he had no reply. After an interval, he knocked and entered – to find the ladies were empty.   In 1976 the whole building vanished.

NOTTINGHAM   The **Classic** in Market St., is close to Lenton Abbey area. Built on the site of a former priory, it dated back to 1875 as a skating rink but morphed into a 3 screen cinema. So the ghost may have been a monk,   but appeared more modern to some. The Paranormal database settles for Pale man. Post cinema days from 1984 a mock medieval tavern was opened, but was that what the ghost wanted?   The building had all gone by 1991.

OXFORD   Playingbingo.co.uk has a section on lost bingo halls. This includes the **Regal,** Cowley, which was eyes down until 2004. A Trafford had his first job there from 1994-97 and was happy there, but claimed it was incredibly haunted. Staff disliked being alone in some parts of the building, and especially the old projection booth, in which the machines had stood idle since 1970. The Gala club was then a "genuinely terrifying place" to be, but as an evangelical church today, is less likely to be so paranormal. But the **Ultimate Picture Palace** (1911) does have a soul – "there is something about it" , says the owner Becky Hallsmith.

WELLINGBOROUGH   The **Lyric/ABC** cinema used to disturb the cleaners after closing time, when a shadowy figure would appear.   Balls of light would also manifest. These balls can be observed on CCTV left on through the night. This continued in bingo days until 1975 when the Lyric Club was demolished and a shopping centre called the Swansgate replaced it. A replacement Lyric bingo club is now a church. A final comment in Picture House no. 3,   1983 sounds a note of cynicism,   as Alan A Ashton was chief projectionist there from 1956-63.   He never saw anything, nor did a man working in the cinema on night maintenance, but people slept in the cinema after he left, hoping to spot "Daniel" as he was nicknamed. He describes the ghost as a put up job to gain publicity.

The Classic, Nottingham   and Danilo, Quinton, Birmingham

The Lyric, Wellingborough

THE NORTH

BARROW –IN- FURNESS

The lavishly appointed **Ritz** cinema built for Union cinemas in 1936 had become an ABC and then a Hutchinson Group
triple. It was last used by **Apollo**, but by then it had acquired not only rats but ghosts, which a five strong team from Phoenix Paranormal Investigations were to encounter shortly after closure in February, 1999. By then a new site had been found by Apollo in Hollywood Park with 6 screens, saving them further subdividing an old building. PPI were rewarded by diverse phenomena over almost 4 hours. Several team members felt physical pain in their limbs, nausea and at the rear of screen 1 upstairs, extreme sadness. A female was heard crying near the foyer, and one psychic spotted a girl of about six crying on the stage of screen 1. She was thin, scared, with hurt emotions – dark hair. Two people sighted orbs, one was captured on digital camera when crossing the screen. Plenty of cold spots, and shadows were observed in specific seats. Mandy also sensed the cinema had been bombed or was on fire, which is interesting, as it was a fire in 2003 that sealed its fate. Geoff felt the left side of his face burning near the organ pit. Far more is in the PPI report, which was covered rather flippantly by the media at the time, but new owners Credo were willing to let them in.

BEVERLEY The **Picture Playhouse** dates from 1865 and had been the Corn Exchange before becoming a cinema in 1911. *Ghosts of Beverley and the East Riding* includes some memories of the unexplained. One ghost can be named. Ernest Symmons, who first set up the cinema and ran it until his death in 1957, and his widow Thelma in charge into the bingo years. Mr Symmons used a button attached to a post on the left side if facing the ports, to code if the focus or sound was right. It was felt he carried on this practice after 1957. The cinema had cold spots, one so severe that a man called Adrian found himself temporarily glued to the spot. This was in 1988, while staff were clearing up after bingo. But it could work out for the best , as a colleague visiting the bank felt he must go into the Playhouse for no obvious reason. It was only when he found a milk pan burning dry in the upper office that he knew why he had been "summoned" A projectionist also received help in the cooling of an overheated rectifier (this converts AC current to DC) as even with an electrician it looked like the children would never see the end of the show. Another man in the box named Paul distinctly heard the comment –"Good Focus" above the sound of the projection. However he soon found, after a search of the area, that neither Paul, the assistant manager or anyone else had contacted the box. The Playhouse is now Brown's department store, after finally closing as a cinema in 2004, so the remark will not be made again.

Also in Beverley, the **Regal** boasted a ballroom floor, which "it" used to cross. A fatal fall happened in the 1760s when the original Assembly rooms were built, and the 18th century fabric was incorporated into the cinema. "It" came back with a vengeance during a general election, when ballot boxes had to be guarded overnight by a policeman and Tom, both in sleeping bags. They were startled by footsteps walking across the floor, up the stage steps then a loud bang – but nobody was found and no figure was observed by the men. Demolished in 1998, there are flats on the site so no ballroom floor to walk on today.

The Regal Ballroom and the Playhouse

Gaumont, Halifax turns to Liquid

HALIFAX   Back in 1948 the audience saw a flash of red before the film – *The Ghost of Frankenstein* cut out. Upstairs the projection room was on fire and 25 years old Raymond Farrar had no chance. A full six decades later staff at the Liquid nightclub see a man walk through walls, but regulars at the old **Gaumont** cinema and later bingo club know who it is. As a proud new father, Raymond would have had a problem finding peace, so who else would it be? See the Halifax Courier for more information.

KEIGHLEY   The **Picture House** is one of our earliest cinemas (1913). It was also equipped with a small stage. Otherwise an actress would not have committed suicide by throwing herself from the balcony. The Paranormal database says that from 1996, filmgoers had seen a woman, some said in period dress, open a fire door. But staff found the door secure. The cinema is now twinned and updated, although screen 1 may still feel a bit uneasy. But at least there is no balcony to re-enact that suicide from.

POCKLINGTON   The **Ritz,** now an Arts centre, was formerly a unique mix of cinema and slot machine museum. The loft was once used for cock fights, so manageress Kath Tatterton might have seen a fleeing bird, but the sound effects over the pay box included babbling water, a social gathering, disembodied footsteps and banging, while the cleaner came off worse by being struck on the nose. Films are still shown.

ROTHERHAM   An old lady fell to her death from the **Classic** cinema balcony.   Shoulders were tapped, skirts tugged, the   lights came back on. During twinning in 1978, a foreman painter sensed weight on his ladder as he painted a ceiling. He stayed up there, brush in hand! Luckily, the painters outnumbered the ghost who moved to the snooker hall until they left. (But was that open in 1978?-author)   The staff grew used to her, so declined the chance of a priestly exorcism. Perhaps further subdivision drove the ghost away as the old theatre/cinema is now split between a nightclub and a snooker hall with new access from the street.

SCARBOROUGH   A tale of Mabel, a murdered usherette at the former Odeon, was told among staff at the Stephen Joseph Theatre. This was eventually passed on to the public. Only when one bothered to check in the public library was it found no such murder had taken place, and this was a story meant to add colour to the past. Simon Murgatroyd relates this non ghost story online. The morale of this is never invent a ghost with a past that would have made the press.

SHEFFIELD   The Sheffield Paranormal Society have visited the former **Adelphi** Theatre, which was a cinema opened in Attercliffe during 1920. It had later use as a bingo hall, a nightclub and currently a store, but it seems the cause of any activity is put down to a projectionist who loved his job too much. The SPS heard bangings, felt icy cold and saw a curtain twitching. By then cleaners had reported being struck in the toilets and two security guards had left abruptly without saying too much about what they had seen.

SHIPLEY   The **Glen Royal** was used by two bingo companies in the 1990s, and a source with the last company told Bradford Timeline that a lady ghost frequently rushed past him to where the screen was, leaving a cold draught in her wake. Her last rush would have been in January, 2013 when a major fire rendered the cinema unsafe and all was lost, including the art deco time caption floor, above the false ceiling. This was erected to keep the bingo players looking at their score cards!

SWINTON   The **Picture House/Roxy** (1929-65)   now operates as Cafe Sport. A man is seen standing at the end of the bar, but look again and he's gone. Possibly a bit sexist as bottoms are pinched. A shadowy figure is seen between the function room and the toilets.   Project-reveal spent many hours in each room, using EVP, camera and meters, detecting distinct variations in temperature at different levels. Dialogue in these You Tube films can be as hard to pick up as ghostly murmuring, as investigators are dispersed away from a microphone. But their repeat visits suggests summat's up.

1913 as Dated - Keighley Picture House

The Classic, Rotherham   Pocklington Arts centre

THE NORTH EAST

GATESHEAD   The **Askew Picture House** had been built in 1880 but became one the first cinemas in 1913. Cinemas once used "runners" who took film spools on to another cinema. The night watchman was saying he'd heard things that are hard to believe. Two of the runners were spiritualists, who rashly volunteered to spend the night there. By 1am a cold, dank and evil atmosphere prevailed, and after another hour they sensed presences all around them. Messrs Charles Marshall and Joseph Harrap found themselves watching a bizarre play in which a girl wearing a grotesque animal mask danced a gavotte. Two men then fought a spectral dual, enveloped in a ghostly light. Suddenly a girl emerged from the stalls and with a look of pure hatred, raised a pistol at one of the combatants, who then slowly vanished. The night watchman had witnessed these events in less vivid detail, yet Dennis Eadie, the manager had been sceptical. But he recalled an amateur production, c. 1900 in which an actor had been shot. A clown in the play had been charged with murder as he'd threatened Harold Carter but was acquitted through lack of evidence. The real culprit seen in the re-enactment got away with it. Eadie showed a photo to the runners who were sure they'd seen her with the pistol. After she committed suicide and most of the cast were dead, only a play featuring a duel or pistols would trigger a repeat. Or perhaps a film? The Askew was always called Horn's , as Cecil Horn was the first proprietor. It remained with the family. The Salvation Army had put on the plays.

HULL   The **Film theatre** or Hull Screen inside the Central library relocated in 2006. One notable projectionist was Peter who collected films of local interest until his death in 1984. A year later one successor, Jamie, was working at a table near the projectors as a matinee of *A Passage to India* was being shown. He saw the shadow of a man on the wall, then a voice said "Tell Margaret I'm alright." Jamie had never met Peter but guessed it must be him. When Jack, the duty manager related this message to his widow, she found comfort that he was still around, while she was watching that very film.

MIDDLESBROUGH   The **Elite,** later the ABC triple cinema , has more recently saw service as the Crown Bingo Club and then the Crown Pub, until 2015. It was in the last period that the book, *Haunted Teesside* , gives much paranormal detail. The building there before was a Baptist church, and it seems the caretaker perished when the pipes of the boiler he was restocking burst. He felt his work cut short, and maintained a presence in a different era. The association with him was made by staff often hearing keys jingling. Two new managerial staff, struggling to find the right key for a door, 3 nights apart, heard the disembodied comment : "You look a bit lost there, mate".   A little girl of 4 or 5 was more obvious, as the cleaners found small footprints on the floor near the pool tables just after they had washed them down.

Several staff decided to call the ghost Maria, but manager Daniel glimpsed her on TV, and hurried down to find out why a child had been allowed in the pub. Blank looks all round, then, when he rewound the CCTV, nothing was to be seen. Maria was contacted in a séance, and said that neither she or the caretaker would go up to the top floor as a "bad man" was up there. Several rooms were locked up disused, but one was found violently kicked open from inside with the dead bolt still in the locked position, papers strewn about inside. The bad man was only willing to trade insults, but the worst Maria got up was to hide workmen's tools Children's laughter was also heard in the ladies loo, so perhaps Maria had some company but why is/was she still there?

HULL – Tower Cinema – see STOP Press

The ABC without Maria

26

THE NORTH WEST

ACCRINGTON   A good case of vex not the spirits. The main players here, by seniority, are Lucifer, the cinema cat, Mr Gournelle(manager) and Henry, all at the **Classic.** The latter was a workman killed in the 1937 construction of the Odeon, (formerly the Ritz) who caused no trouble – until work began on tripling the cinema. The Manchester Evening News issues for early 1974 record that at first the happenings were low key, such as the curtains closing of their own accord during the midnight showing on an X film. The Tom cat was the initial suspect, but he gave the projection room a wide berth – so much so that when Mr. Gournelle tried to force him into the suite, the panic stricken cat flew down the stairs and clawed an usherette. A workman walking down a corridor felt two icy hands gripping his shoulders, and he fled, never to return. A blue orb hovered in a corridor near to the projection room, where a shadow was also seen. Baffled, a medium was called in (NB the dead contact them, not vice versa). She named the spirit as Henry, who twice angrily said "leave my cinema alone!" Well, such a paragon of respect for an original 1930s cinema should receive honorary membership of the Cinema Theatre Association!. Finally, under strict secrecy, a priest performed an exorcism, and all went quiet thereafter. You will not find Henry or Lucifer in Boots or Specsavers today. In the next town we find an unhappy young man who committed suicide in the orchestra pit.

ALTRINCHAM   Here the Star circuit took over the Hippodrome (1912) in 1963, continuing films upstairs in **Studio 1** and bingo in the stalls. At once footsteps were heard, doors opened and closed, cold patches developed and the tip up seats could stay down unoccupied. The projectors would switch off or on even during a film but were found to be in good working order. Seances were held and spirits contacted but they named no names. The favourite theory was that the ghost was Edward, younger son of Thomas Hargreaves of Rochdale, who owned the Hippodrome, but would only let his son manage but not act there. Ambition thwarted, Edward hung himself. All ended in 1983 when both cinema and club closed and a new office block came in 1987.

BIRKENHEAD   The ABC House or **Savoy** (1938) replaced the older theatre (1864) which has become the Scala in 1921. In this case strange noises have been heard in Rileys Snooker club which took over the stalls area. As customary, the red balls were carefully arranged in triangles, but those on table 10 could be on the floor next day. Better still a young staff member saw an actual apparition. He had asked a woman sitting on a staircase not open to the public to leave. She took no notice but when he and the barman went back nobody was there and no alarm had been triggered. However it is recorded that in music hall days, the lessee's wife , Edith Cole, had tried to clean the kid gloves she wore on stage with a highly inflammable spirit, while smoking at the same time. She may not have died then but may revisit her mistake.

BLACKPOOL   In late 1986 the Blackpool Mail reported strange noises, weird rings of red light, and a smell of fire a week before a real one in Screen 2 of **Studios 1-4.** The firemen at the false alarm found two human shapes on the thermal image intensifier. Police found their dogs would not enter while the projectionist got locked out of his box, and a man entered the ladies toilet and vanished. In the **Royal Pavilion** Cinema workers encountered flickering lights and cold spots. A medium called in said it was a coach driver who had been around in the 1920s. Evidently he drove a motor coach, but his presence is unexplained on the Paranormal database. These cinemas only opened between 1975-87 and are now only partly occupied by Pop World, and presumably uneventful as the Blackpool ghost walk looks at two other cinemas. The **Regent** (1921-71) is now Grade II listed and the false ceilings and alterations over the bingo/snooker years were undone. A photograph online shows a figure in a long dark coat in the disused theatre when there was nobody in shot. In February, 2016, 20 ghost followers not only picked up on this dark malevolent spirit who made them feel sick or trapped but also a mother and her six year daughter, who told a psychic she was called Charlotte. Perhaps the next visit might discover more. The **Empire** was a cinema from 1929-59, but stories of the uncanny relate to its time as a bingo club. The shadow of a man, the sound of a woman crying and a child appearing in the balcony are the main phenomena here. One newspaper dubbed Blackpool Blackghoul!

CHESTER　　Now a bingo hall, the **Gaumont** Cinema, (1931-61) which has a pseudo Tudor frontage, still keeps old George, who is blamed for crashes, bumps and thumps, but can also appear in a brown tweed jacket up in the balcony, He is included on the discoverchester site. No doubt his view is reduced by the false ceiling in the Mecca club.

CREWE　　Before **Apollo** moved In and created a triple cinema (with bingo hall on the ground floor), the building was a dance hall., but before that was the Plaza then Gaumont cinema until 1961. But by the time live music took over in 2006 , the new **M Club** was beset by the sound of heavy footsteps, people's names being called from nowhere, feelings of being watched or worse, objects flying about by themselves. Objects would disappear and reappear. The Club used the ground floor and screen 1 as a recording studio. But the remainder of the building was left untouched in Apollo cinema colours. A group named Spirit Cheshire investigated, and almost at once a sensitive saw an old lady crossing the dance floor towards the stage. The owner had heard about this before, so this came as no surprise, nor that a projection room felt uneasy. On the higher level a man was sensed in screen 3, but not threatening the visitors, just observing them. This group knew nothing of what earlier psychic groups had sensed but they felt uneasy in the same spots. But in 2010 the M Club had to make way for major development. As usual, this was delayed so the cinema stood empty for years.

DIDSBURY   A haunting at the **Capitol** Cinema (1931-56) which became the ABC TV Studios, began in 1958, as an actor, Gareth Jones (35) was due to play someone having a heart attack in the TV series Armchair Theatre. Sadly he died in his dressing room during the performance and his role was hastily rewritten. This was clearly enough to bring him back to haunt the studios for 40 years — long after Armchair Theatre had moved on. However, the old cinema was demolished and perhaps the replacement flats -Capitol Court did not appeal to Gareth.

LIVERPOOL   The city was honoured with a visit from the Most Haunted team, who confirmed that the former Dingle **Gaumont** (1937) was indeed most haunted. A radio presenter had asked how many spirits were there and was told six, but they were all being impeded by a very dark force. Strange lights, and shadowy figures including an audience watching a film on a non -existent screen, and of course there had been deaths here. A bingo player had a heart attack —this would be after 1966, and a man had hung himself behind the screen and resents anyone approaching the site. You Tube has the episode in which the team are suitably spooked, including when a table they are touching falls off the stage.   But it was staff who challenged a man seen in the cellar, who promptly disappeared — he should have done this for Most Haunted! Top Rank closed the bingo club in 1998, and the art deco interior was left to decay except for some rock groups practising inside — one wonders how well this went down with Dark Spirit, but perhaps he/it can only control the dead. The Most Haunted team claim that the physical body has an auric field, and no spirit can enter it without your permission. Mediums may cautiously give that permission. As one cinema employee claimed over half the cinemas he worked in had a resident ghost, perhaps 40 or more of the 82 in Liverpool on the Cinema Treasures website should get a book to themselves!

Lucifer never went in here

Studio 1, Altrincham

Hilda, an usherette, saw a lady ghost in a purple veil float down the stairs in the **Grand Cinema**, Lancaster c 1938. It is now open as a theatre. (Lancs Eve Post, 5/3/2009

The Century, Cheam showing the stage

"I won't sell!" – but the Astoria, Streatham was built
in 1929

THE LONDON AREA

ACTON Playing Bingo mentions a ghost called Horace who hung himself in the projection room in cinema days, when it was the **Savoy,** not the Mecca. That room could never be got warm, and some felt uneasy working in the club, but overall there was a happy team there. Demolition came in 1996.

BARNET The **Everyman** (formerly the Odeon) has digital projection now but in the 1980s the cinema had two Victoria 8s. The projectionist was standing between them, idly watching the audience leave through the porthole, when he saw a couple behind him reflected in the glass. Smartly dressed, he in a dark suit, she in a long red coat, the projectionist promised to be with them in a minute. But the visitors had vanished, and they would have had to pass the staff room to get to the box. But a colleague in there had seen nothing. Who they were and why they headed to the box is a mystery.

CAMBERWELL   A much worse experience befell Jane Smith who came from a Wiltshire village to visit her elder sister, Helen. But by the summer of 1973 the **Odeon** had fallen on hard times, and not all levels were open. Jane wanted the ladies halfway through the film in the upper balcony, and she was told it was off the foyer. She soon became lost and descended another flight of stairs to a dimly lit corridor. At last she spied a ladies sign. The toilets seemed dilapidated, and no sooner had she found a cubicle than loud footsteps were heard approaching and not muffled by the three sets of doors between the stairs and the toilets. Someone entered and went to the last cubicle, but Jane was alarmed to hear a man sobbing and weeping in great distress. By then her sister was asking a staff member where Jane was. Reunited, two staff members said the lower loos had been disused for years, and their search revealed nothing, and an exit beyond was sealed up. Helen's husband said nothing when the women returned, but later told his wife of the story of a middle aged man who had hanged himself from a pipe over a cubicle before the 1960s when his projectionist friend worked there. Staff had run into this ghost all round the cinema including in the auditorium. However, the Odeon closed in 1975 and was finally demolished in 1993.

CHEAM   Also long demolished, several managers mistook phantom footfalls heard crossing the **Century's** stage area for intruders. Was this the workman who disappeared during the construction without collecting his wages? His lunchbag and coat were left hanging where the stage was to be. Staff got used to the sounds and would say "There goes Charlie again" In 1955 three reporters from the Epsom Herald held a vigil, heard the shuffling footsteps but found nothing. Century was a name used by Granada for their second run houses. Century House (offices) marks the site today.

EUSTON   The somewhat down at heel **Tolmer** cinema (named after the square) was affectionately described in Picture House no. 40, 2015. A church which gave up the ghost after the Great War was turned into a cinema and looked more like one when the spire was removed in 1929. But the last minister had hung himself over the altar so the church had to be deconsecrated. Handyman and night watchman Henry Clark was the obvious witness, who saw a bright light moving from the altar area to the foyer, then disappearing. This being around 4am, it was time for Mr Clark to take tea at Euston station. How often this happened is unclear, but clearly it cannot today. Farewells were made in March, 1972, when the double bill included "Die slowly – you'll enjoy it more" How appropriate.

NOTTINGHILL GATE   The Historian Richard Jones wrote "Walking Haunted London" in 1999, and he found an unquiet cashier at the **Coronet** cinema.   When it had been a successful theatre a cashier was caught in the early 1900s stealing from the till at Christmas.   To escape the manager she rushed up to the gods and threw herself off the balcony. Thereafter staff meetings were disturbed by re-enactments and moved lower down.   Footsteps going upwards can be heard, especially round Christmas, but for variety, tins of paint for use in a redecoration were moved about.

PECKHAM   Staff in the **Tower** Cinema (1914-56) noticed a figure walking 10 feet off the ground. This was the level of a chapel previously on the site. More sightings were made of a figure in period clothes, and one of two upholsterers refused to work there again, after hours. Clearly a non smoker, packs of cigarettes were ruined by water, when there were no pipes above them or rain outside. More dangerous some scaffolding just erected collapsed. All so far recorded in the book *"Haunted London"* As a finale before the main cinema was replaced by a car park, several workmen quit in haste after seeing figures pass through walls A shortened part of the original 100 foot tower was left as a gateway.

The Danilo, Quinton has become the Reel,

but the Empire Blackpool has gone to Eyes Down

Cancan legs move from Headington to Brighton,

The Lyric, Carmarthen

Moray Playhouse, Elgin

The Palace Cinema, Devizes with Angel Bingo too

Entering the Empire, Hemel Hempstead, and a ghost cam in
Radio Lincolnshire

The long closed
Vogue in Stoke
Newington seen
in my dream

The
second
Odeon in
Brighton

ABC used cladding to update in Mansfield, and the "terrifying" Regal, Cowley

The Torbay at Paignton

Blackie standing in for Lucifer, the Cinema Cat

Disturbing the spirits? The Granville, Ramsgate

STOKE NEWINGTON   No the **Vogue** has no known ghost, but held the London record for being shuttered and unused for 40 years until late 2000. The author had assumed this was still the case, but dreamt that workmen had opened up and were inside. Hours later, with a party of passing cinema enthusiasts, he saw his dream fulfilled and is still puzzled why. A Turkish restaurant is inside.

STREATHAM   A large Victorian residence was demolished to make way for the magnificent new cinema, the **Astoria.** The owner, Edward Frederick Janes had refused to sell for years, so attached was he to Chesterfield house. But two weeks after the grand opening in June, 1930, Janes died, maybe of a broken heart. On Christmas night 1933, Lewis Amis, the fireman had reached the tea lounge, when he saw a figure approaching. His torch revealed not a burglar but an elderly man in a long white gown with a wizened wrinkled face and a short beard. The figure swept on through two massive closed fire doors into the stalls and reached the stage. He then announced to the petrified fireman "I won't sell!" This meant nothing to Amis, nor who had lived on the site, but when the apparition was described to Janes' widow, everything including the beard matched her late husband. This account came from the writings of local historian John W Brown in 2002, but he does not say this is still occurring in the barely recognisable eight screen Odeon there today.

WORCESTER PARK The Odeon's uneventful history was broken by the suicide of a projectionist. When the **Odeon** closed in 1956, It became Gateway supermarket. One butcher there was curious about what was beyond the false walls and above the ground floor. He managed to reach the balcony up a ladder and then the projection room. A newspaper was still there dated the day the suicide happened. Older workmates confirmed the cinema's staircase and projection room had been haunted and one manager would never go upstairs alone. Bob related this to Mawgrim's World. And how come the suicide? Because the Odeon was closing and the project-ionist could not bear losing his job.

GREENFORD A late discovery, the **Granada** (1937-66) was a little out of centre so not as busy as some. A ghost dubbed "Charlie" startled the staff and seemed annoyed when the staff room was used. Was Charlie carried forward from the Catholic Church on the site before, or more important did he adapt to the Tesco store that followed on from the Granada?

An iron foundry preceded the Odeon, Ashford

Turkish baths lost out to the ABC, Brighton

The Odeon, Aylesbury - perplexity in a multiplex

ASHFORD (Kent) Not all manifestations are visible. After the bingo players have left their tables at the **Mecca** (ex Odeon), a manager told us the temperature can drop, and the sound of clanking chains is heard at the stage end. This might be related to the cinema being built over a former iron foundry where one worker is still too busy for 41 years of eyes down.

AYLESBURY As the original Odeon languished derelict, the successor **ABC then Odeon** ran into problems according to the Bucks Herald . By 2003, cinema staff were convinced screen 5 felt different to the other 5 screens. One usher sensed someone up behind him, then the lights went out instead of dimming. On the screen a face appeared oval shaped with a mouth but no eyes. After that this screen was entered in pairs, as guests seemed to be still there after the film, but were not. If anything can explain this, the Odeon is near the Crown Court, outside which hangings once took place. The author was lucky when he saw a film alone in there, as it was neither unnaturally cold or smelling of rotting flesh, but he went early in the day.

BEACONSFIELD A long deceased manager (Walter Gay) with a dislike of supernatural films was blamed by the resident manager, Ms Clair Matthews, who had to substitute *Baby* for *Ghostbusters* in March, 1985. An amplifier blew on the opening night, light bulbs blew in the foyer, and a quarter ton projector was moved out of its position, missing the screen. Loud crashing and shuffling noises kept Clair awake. Earlier, when the Exorcist was shown, the curtains closed on it!! Perhaps the manager mingled with the audience unnoticed as just another thin grey haired man, but then several usherettes were scared out of the job, so they left. . But as a Prezzo restaurant today, all traces of the past have gone.

BRIGHTON   *Haunted theatres of East Sussex* includes the **ABC,** which opened as the Savoy in 1930 This cinema preserved the memory of the Turkish bathhouse it replaced, as it became common for cleaners and other staff to hear sounds of water echoing round the building, and steam appearing from nowhere. Having a car park underneath may have helped, but since closure in 1999 the cinema has been put to multiple use. The well known **Duke of Yorks** cinema also replaced an earlier brewery, and one wall was incorporated. Cleaning and security staff, working alone, but not audiences, have smelt beer being brewed. This may be due to a brewery worker working alone being crushed to death by a fall of barrels, with nobody to help him. Given the name Tim, the ghost is thought benevolent. Paranormal Database speculates he may also haunt the nearby Fire Station, perhaps because the brewery extended that way. Much more modern is the present **Odeon** (1973), a conversion of a conference Centre and skating rink. Local legend says a man called George was killed during the construction, and a manager saw him standing at the top of a flight of stairs, while to gain attention, he may tap guests on the shoulder.

CHATHAM   Behind the former Woolworths store was Fullaghers Yard, where the **Invicta** once stood. This had closed as a cinema in 1939 and was used by the Church Army as a wartime hostel. But a bomb fell, killing four, three of them children. It later became an indoor market, an entertainment centre, where the Rolling Stones played in 1974, and finally until 1985 a bingo hall. But children's voices were inexplicably heard. And staff saw a man in green uniform walking round the foyer and up in the balcony. Who was he? A psychic was asked and came up with Bill Malan, who sure enough was a cinema commissionaire from 1940 until his death in 1955, but not at this ex cinema! The phenomena died down but has been recorded by Andrew Green on www.mystical.co.uk

EAST GRINSTEAD   The former Radio Centre and latterly **Cannon** had an impeccably dressed manager, Mr Christopher, who died in the 1950s. But twenty years later an usherette (Mrs Chamberlain) spied a man in full evening dress leaning over the balcony. Before she could ask him to sit down he slowly faded away. Other staff also saw him, and he seems to be versatile as the sound of coal being shovelled at night was heard after it became a morning job. Worse, a huge pin in the boiler door became loose in January, 1970 and it took 5 men to replace it. It took even more to demolish the cinema in 1990 and build the Atrium Centre incorporating twin cinemas.

FOLKESTONE   In 1941, heavy bombing raids closed the **Savoy,** Folkestone, and these can be blamed for the fall of a ventilation motor on top of a boy there with his mother. But it was not the boy but his distraught mother who disturbed the staff in future years. Only building workers could notice now.

Who was Martha - an usherette?

GRAVESEND   Martha, a ghost who liked to crash the seats

after the show in the **Plaza**, had found peace as all was quiet by the time the cinema closed in 1955, leaving the seats to Joan and Audrey, so the hairdressers and carpet retailers will hear nothing today.

HASTINGS   The Gaiety theatre (1882-1932) attracted a man of difficult disposition, who stayed on when a cinema, latterly the **ABC, then Odeon** took residence. He found fellow theatregoers unclean and undesirable. To remove those in front of him, he would tap them on the shoulder and ask them to be quiet. Tiring of this unfair complaint, they would eventually move, as he laughed hysterically. In the 1970s and early eighties a person in the wrong seat would get the same treatment. While this could continue after twinning, it seems to have faded away in the quad Hastings has today.

HEMEL HEMPSTEAD   The town's second Odeon has become the Cineworld, Jarmans Park. Perhaps it attracted a poltergeist as one room has objects flying through the air and the sound of moaning. One hopes the room is not one of the screens. The nightclub is also paranormally active.

ROSEHILL   The Top Rank Club/Mecca   in this New Malden suburb had previously been the **Gaumont**. If deaths cause haunting, this cinema had a full quota. A night watchman was found dead, a builder was killed and a boilerman fell down steps to his death. During re-wiring in 1972, an electrician greeted a figure standing in a doorway without success. The figure slowly dissolved. This grey figure did the same for the cleaners. One account says an organist collapsed and died at the console. He was seen about the bingo club, and doors opened and shut —a crime during play as bingo halls are more hushed than churches. Residents reported loud organ music, c. 1957 – after the organ had gone! Sixty years later, Mecca play on here.

ST ALBANS   In 2014, The former **Odeon**, was reincarnated as the Odyssey, hopefully without any area being unpleasant to enter. The manager's dog used to refuse to go into screen 3, but the cinema is one screen again. A trainee projectionist told Mawgrim's World his chief advised him not to go down to the boiler house alone, ostensibly because you could fall down the steps and not be missed until the film failed to start. One day, no other person was available, so he told people where he was going and for how long. Coming back up he felt he was being watched malevolently, and that two points of intense heat were boring into him. Staff even tossed a coin to see who would chain up the exit doors after closing – but nobody knew of anything untoward that might explain their experiences.

ST LEONARDS The Silverhill Working Mens Club occupies space used by an early cinema that closed to competition around 1922. . The ticket booth was at the club entrance, and the steep stairs to the function room led to where films were shown. One keyholder was totally sceptical about ghosts, even after seeing one. Living nearby he could attend when a burglar alarm went off. In autumn 2003, he attended at night and brought his dog, just in case. Ascending the steep staircase together, the dog froze in terror, for standing at the top was a man in a suit and peaked cap, evidently checking tickets. He boldly continued, until the figure dissolved and his dog returned to normal. But what devotion to duty for tickets to be checked 80 to 90 years after the last film!

SITTINGBOURNE As if the **Queens**, did not have enough problems without a haunting, but this was formerly a brewery. In the 1890s a man fell into a beer vat in the cellar, and his presence was sensed by a former manager. But a swirling mist in the foyer had natural causes – a steam laundry in an adjacent alley was to blame!

TANKERTON The Cinema Organ Society reported that the heirs to the **Troc,** the fire brigade, heard organ music, which is odd as even the C.O.S. did not know about any organ installation. That goes one better than at Rosehill.

TUNBRIDGE WELLS An employee changing the canopy of the **Ritz** in Tunbridge Wells lost his balance and fell to his death. His ghost was seen subsequently. Most intriguing of all, and a rare event, was a case of time slip in the **Kosmos**, According to the 1970 issue of "Man, Myth and Magic", a Mrs Charlotte was out shopping with her husband, After they split up, the lady noticed a passage next to a shop she had used in

Calverley Road. She walked into a room panelled in dark mahogany, lit by frosted glass shades. Two women in rather long dresses and men in dark lounge suits were seated talking. However, there was no sound and no smell of coffee either. Mrs Charlotte told her husband about her discovery, but they were unable to find the café. on returning a week later. Nobody knew of it, until the club steward at the Constitutional Club recalled there was such a room in the old Kosmos Cinema, closed in 1960, but all had been absorbed into a self service store. One wonders what would have happened if Mrs Charlotte had ordered coffee, asked for a newspaper, and paid in modern currency, but a family on holiday in France found a "bargain" old fashioned hotel and actually stayed the night – and that is even rarer. Perhaps a cinema enthusiast would welcome a time slip! But more common would be a time anomaly, where a building plays back sounds from a past era, such as at the Mecca, Ashford.

Crawley ABC   Chatham Invicta

ANONYMOUS The Mawgrim's World website- visit (www. mawgrim.co.uk) has several tales, including one from an unspecified Kent multiplex opened in 1999. Here a murder also took place but in the old house that preceded the cinema. Something odd is seen in screen 6, where a man lingers after the film, or even appears before the audience are seated. He vanishes suddenly if approached by staff, when the only unlocked exit involves passing them. Music CDs can play up and lights flicker unaccountably. Pre the digital age audiences complained of a shadow interrupting the projector beam, but nobody could physically squeeze between the lens and the pane of glass. This multiplex seems to be thriving with or without its extra patron. One wonders what films the apparition prefers or avoids! And are you wondering where we are? – a clue is Eureka!.or a trinity of KFC, McDs and Burger King!

DOVER? Yes the manager of the **Plaza**, George Roberts was killed with a blow by an axe and money taken. But the young culprit, a projectionist, was tried and sentenced to death in 1941, commuted to penal servitude. Unlike in Bristol, the case was resolved and no ghost story is recorded. For cinema murders see Picture House, no. 38, 2013.

RAMSGATE? The **Granville** was a theatre between 1947 and 1991, but now is twinned as a cinema with theatre use in one auditorium. Very detailed information is found on Thanet Ghostwatch website. They have since paid several visits, but the paranormal activity primarily dates back to theatre days. It was noticeable that switching round the ladies and gents toilets had suppressed activity (confusion?) and an usherette revealed she could not move seats installed since her lifetime.

THE SOUTH

ALDERSHOT   The manager of a brand new **Cineworld** which only opened in October, 2012, hardly expected to come across a ghost. An interesting film on You Tube entitled *Haunted cinema* has the hands on and named staff going to the extent of handing complimentary tickets to guests who felt uncomfortable in screen 3. A construction worker had died when the cinema was being built, so we are told, before hearing an usher, whose last customer had vanished during the credits. But sadly all this was a Warner promotion for the film "The Conjuring" then on release in Cineworld. Perhaps the give away is a cinema routinely refunding tickets to guests coming out of a screen, rather than closing it "for cleaning"

COSHAM   The events that set up the paranormal in the now demolished **Carlton** (1934) took place in December, 1940. Heavy bombing not only put the cinema out of action for a year, but killed the chief projectionist. The cellars were used for keeping the dead and wounded from the vicinity. By the time Mike Whitcombe arrived in 1999, he worked alone in the box for many hours. He sensed a presence and talked to someone he expected was the man killed 60 years earlier. A man called Tim came to the box, and spoke about the former chief, and it became clear Tim was not a wind up but a spirit medium, who had been contacted. Days before Mike had gone to sort out a sound problem in screen 3 , leaving a lately arrived film hastily wound onto a spool. When he returned, the film had been rewound to a maker's join he had missed. The medium was already aware of this event

But later when the former chief took a dislike to another projectionist, he scared him out of the job by bobbins and splicing tape being thrown at him. That was his last shift!.

Meanwhile, the boiler room was unnerving engineers there to fix the boiler. They felt they were being watched. Years earlier a meter man refused to enter, so the sceptical chief told him he'd bring his dog. But the dog ran from the building and would not go back. Mike enjoyed his posting, in spite of the odd event causing a shiver down his spine.

CRAWLEY   Possibly the only former Shipman and King Cinema to be included in this book. **The Embassy,** later Cannon, later ABC, became a Bar Med in 2000. But it was business as usual for the ghosts, who included a little girl, who used to appear after the film ended. Bar staff were now pelted with light bulbs in the former projection room. The Crawley News awarded a spooky score of 5, one ahead of Asda with four. Poltergeists inflate your score. But demolition, as here, may reduce it to zero.

GOSPORT   No ghost story here, but it is interesting to record that the Ritz was saved by a medium, Peter Walker, who re-opened the cinema against the financial odds, thanks to his spirit guides. An issue of Mercia Newsreel no. 8, 1986, records this, but Mr Walker was never able to expand, and after other operators took over, the Ritz was replaced by a branch of Iceland after 2001.

PORTSLADE   The former **Rothbury** Cinema (1934-64) lacks any architectural charm, but bingo players gave way to broadcasters. Now Heart FM, staff and visitors are known to experience cold spots, strange lights and phantom footsteps. In 1990, an interview with Betty Shine was interrupted by a power cut and the failure of backup systems, all except in the Studio itself.

PORTSMOUTH   Before Cosham, (q.v.) Mike Whitcombe had worked in the WR Glen designed **ABC**, which came off lightly in the dockland bombing. Despite this, screen 2 always felt a little uneasy. Some men cleaning the foyer carpets overnight gave up as a presence in screen 2 kept closing the auditorium doors and hindering their work. Soon after Mike and another colleague were seated outside screen 2 waiting for a third man to finish, when they both saw the door hook rise and the door shut by itself, saving them the trouble. They hastily moved outside, but strangely, no paranormal finale was put on for Mike when he returned to strip out the building after closure in 2000. Demolition followed in 2002.

NEWBURY Just received, Ben Doman's account of a new cleaner starting in the Forum/ABC, which had films in the 484 seat circle from 1982. She was deemed capable of finishing off the stairs on her own, but a second cleaner joined her and just smiled and hummed as she worked. Back in the staff room the novice asked where this lady was, as she had gone through an exit door to the car park. Puzzled, the cleaners asked for a description. This matched a colleague who had died mid shift a week ago! Visibly shaken, her replacement was sent home, and decided not to return to this job

The Rothbury is Heart FM Radio

The Ritz, Gosport

The Savoy/ABC, Portsmouth before the bombing

BARNSTAPLE   Paranormal database gives the name Fred to the spirit who has been seen this century. Whether name or nickname, a man fell from the roof during repair work in 1931. This was when the present **Central** cinema opened as the Gaumont Palace. Now with Scott Cinemas, it is Grade II listed.

**Little Theatre Cinema ,
Bath**

Central, Barnstaple

BATH Torchlight Paranormal Investigations were able to confirm, in late 2013 what staff of the **Little Theatre Cinema** already knew about this art house gem. The team picked up strange sounds, a distinct feel of a presence about screen 2 and the stage area of Screen 1. Working late here can be a bit disquieting, the Bath Chronicle reported.

BRISTOL A former naval officer, Robert Parrington Jackson, came as manager of the **Odeon** in 1946, but soon after he had collected the takings from the box office to his own office, a shot rang out and the manager was found shot in the temple. He died next day (May 30th, 1946) and it was thought significant 5 shots had just run out on screen in *The light that failed.* Theories explaining the untouched money included that the killer had panicked or that the manager was a ladies' man confronted by an angry lover or husband. There was a death bed confession by Billy Fisher, a crook from South Wales, but no arrests were ever made. This may explain cold spots, unexplained feelings and a few times his apparition in the cinema, but in 1985 the interior was realigned within the original shell, incorporating three screens. Confusing to haunt, in these circumstances. In the Fortean Times it is claimed that the priest Lionel Fanthorpe was called in to give the Odeon an exorcism. Paranormal Database adds more to the mix, by claiming staff have seen people milling about the auditorium (all of them?) who disappear when approached. One seat in screen 3 is said to be home to a shadowy apparition, but was he murdered?

The **Kings** Cinema was once ABC's main house in the city, and there is a story of an unknown suicide by someone leaping from the balcony. But the Kings was replaced by the Housing department and it is one of the rest areas there that has a chill which is thought to recall the half forgotten event.

DEVIZES   The **Palace** (1912) cinema merits a place on hauntedplaces.org **as** it offers two apparitions in period clothing, who have been seen in the lounge and on the staircase. The projection booth is also haunted with the feel of an unseen presence and cold spots. Nobody frequents a cinema more in life than the projectionist. Staff also hear loud footsteps.

PAIGNTON   Apparently author Agatha Christie used to sit in the balcony of the **Torbay** cinema, in row 2 seat 2, calling it the Gaiety in her novels. But it is not her but Mr W Farrant Gilly, a showman and cinema promoter who returns here. He used to smoke a cigar and the air in the circle was impregnated with the unmistakable smell, although no smoke was visible. The cinema has closed, affected by a multiplex but the Paignton Picture House Trust bought the cinema late in 2015 and hope to restore it to glory.

PLYMOUTH   The present **Reel** cinema had been opened by ABC in 1938, and survived the blitz. So did several spirits, some hailing from several burial grounds in the Derry's Cross area. Screen 2 seems to be the epicentre, with a woman known as Emily, who was an actress in the previous theatre, who committed suicide in her dressing room. Audiences see a lady in 1940s dress sitting in the front row. Look again and she has disappeared, but those taking "her" seat can feel nauseous and uneasy. Door knockings and loud noises are heard in the ladies loo but not in the gents. Kevin Hynes has an account of paranormal investigations in April 2006 and October, 2009. Hidden Realms were also there in 2007, and a man they identified as George was frantically searching for his wife and children. He gave the impression of not realising he was dead. So were all the family by then, but the psychic saw the wife and children standing at a graveside, so something like a fire on the site seems to have separated them. How do you tell a spirit they are dead?

The later to be Reel cinema triple in Plymouth

QUOTE : Sara Chiappa of the Caledonian Paranormal Investigations team said that you do not have to have a death in a cinema for it to be haunted.

SCOTLAND

CLYDEBANK   In March, 2016, Safedem began to demolish the disused La Scala/ABC, which had been a landmark and survived the blitz. Bingo in the stalls outlived the final cinema in the balcony (1969-83) but one of the bingo club employees recalled it was a scary place at night. A grey lady walked about and the middle of the hall near the staircase was cold all year round. Four staff were alarmed by knocking under the stage, and hurried outside.. In wartime the cinema was a refuge and many were killed in the blitz nearby, but who may have sought a surviving building to haunt.

La Scala in busier days

EDINBURGH   The UK's largest theatre was previously a super cinema. Not everyone knows that the Arthur bar in the **Playhouse** is named after the well established ghost of a maintenance manager. Nor that one of many uncanny coincidences associated with the film *The Exorcist* happened at the *Cameo.* One late showing sold 333 tickets at £2 each. Do the maths! A woman may haunt the **Filmhouse,** (1831) but the Paranormal Database has no further information.

ELGIN   The **Moray Playhouse** dates from 1932, and now has a side entrance and 3 screens. It seems the extra third screen added in 2015 disturbed spirits already there. No visuals, but staff can feel watched, or the cleaners say someone seems to be walking behind them. The manager Martin Thomson thought he heard someone entering the toilets but nobody came out again. Only a proper paranormal investigation could explain what might have happened to trigger these phenomena.

MOTHERWELL   You will be a Lidl late, if looking for the former **Rex/ABC** -21 years to be precise. A man nicknamed Oscar for film reasons had a reputation for scaring away usherettes about 60 years ago, and could have come from the previous theatre on the site. By May, 1962, staff were saying rows they had cleaned with the sprung loaded seats in the upright position were lowering as if patrons were using them. Nobody was caught trying to trick them. Loud bangings were heard in the auditorium. The manager asked Tom Robertson to investigate. He definitely picked up on a presence, but half suspected the manager saw a ghost as a publicity asset. Mr Robertson felt a dusty storeroom was the most likely place to stage a sit in. By then the Motherwell Times had been alerted and sent three young reporters to sit in on the vigil in the room, locked from inside, with the external windows taped. Despite this, the psychic was amazed and the reporters terrified to find a shaft of light transformed into a gleaming skull, and kept doing so after a torch was turned off again. The reporters wrote up their experience, but the manager had calculated that having Oscar around would help business and on the whole this proved correct. The psychic got a free pass as a reward, but was told he was over using it and it was soon torn up!

STORNAWAY /STEOMAGHAGH *Jesus Christ Superstar* was released in 1973. The film met none of the problems of *the Life of Brian* but pop music was regarded as heathen in the island's Presbyterian free church, so this was one blasphemous film the Playhouse should not show. It did screen the film, ah but the **Playhouse** was not struck by lightning or burnt down, but locals were convinced a minister had cursed it, rather than believe the fire regs had not been complied with, hastening closure. Until 2015 it was used by the Royal British Legion, who reluctantly found the space uneconomic.

A ghost vigil on the top floor – Motherwell ABC

The Hapless Playhouse, Stornaway /Steomaghagh

WALES

BUCKLEY / BWCLE   The former theatre then cinema, dating from 1925, has been claimed as Wales' most haunted. Manager Leighton Openshaw was welcomed into the job when a glass was thrown at him. Later he saw a man hanging on a CCTV monitor, and so did several colleagues called to confirm the sighting. Nothing was found upstairs, and when everyone returned the monitor was back to normal. It was known that a projectionist had been killed in a fire in 1946, but staff thought there were several other spirits – a mix of the good, bad and the mischievous.

A strong Most Haunted contender in Flintshire

A ghost hunter's diary of the visit by PRUK in 2010 reports a medium had the impression that the dead projectionist was a non smoker, but a colleague may have left a cigarette not properly extinguished. Among the unpleasant entities in residence was a former murderer who was not caught but became an executioner, obviously well before 1925. A man with the same name had killed himself, his wife, brother and children Frederick (12) and Louisa (8) the children appearing to the group. In December, 2014, the Most Haunted team were invited and from clips shown by the Daily Express found the Tivoli a scary place with no go areas.

CARMARTHEN/ CAERFYDDIN   The current auditorium of the **Lyric** dates from 1936, and is currently a live theatre with some film shows. The Paranormal database quoting a former member of staff, says that several figures, male and female have been seen since early days. More specifically, in 1996 a tall man in a suit was seen in the projection room. We do not have a photo of that area, but the pay box is rather special. The Creepy Carmarthen tour is well regarded, but focuses on older properties in this ancient Welsh town. A newer one is the Vue (formerly Apollo Cinema) the first in Wales to be purpose built for digital projection.

AN A-Z OF CINEMAS STILL OPEN

ASHFORD (Kent) Cineworld, Eureka Entertainment Centre, TN25 4BN

AYLESBURY Odeon, Cattle Market, Exchange St, HP20 1UK

BARNSTAPLE Central, 77, Boutport St., EX31 1SR

BATH Little Theatre, St Michael's Place, BA1 1SF

BEDFORD Aspects Leisure Park, Newnham Avenue MK41 9LW

BELPER Ritz 76B, King St., DE56 1QA

BRIGHTON Duke of York's Preston Circus, BN1 4NR

BRIGHTON Odeon, 17 West St., BN1 2RL

BRISTOL Odeon, Union St., BS1 2DS

DEVIZES Palace, 19-20 Market Place, SN10 1JQ

EDINBURGH Playhouse, 18-22 Greenside Place, EH1 3AA

ELGIN Moray Playhouse 199 High St., IV30 1DJ

HASTINGS Odeon, Queens Road, TN34 1QP

HEMEL HEMPSTEAD Cineworld, Jarman Park, HP2 4J W

IPSWICH   Film Theatre, Corn Exchange,   King St., IP1 1D

KEIGHLEY   Picture House, North St.,   BD21 3AF

KETTERING   Odeon, Pegasus Court, Wellingborough Rd.,
NN13 6XS

LANCASTER   Vue,   Church St.,   LA1 1LP

LEAMINGTON SPA   Vue,   Portland Place,   CU32 5EP

LONDON AREA

Barnet Everyman   Barnet Hill, EN5 1AB
Nottinghill Gate   Coronet   103, Nottinghill Gate, W11 3LB
Streatham   Odeon, 47-49 High Road, SW16 1PW

LUTON   Cineworld,   Galaxy Centre,   Bridge St.,   LU1 2NB

PLYMOUTH   Reel,   Derry's Cross, PL1 2SW

ST ALBANS Odyssey,   166, London Road, AL1 1PQ

THE MOST HAUNTED BY TOWN

South - 3 cinemas close by

North - 4 cinemas close by

One being the ABC, Brighton

One being the Regent, Blackpool

The apparitions who
were visible for the
longest duration and
were most revealing
factually, took stage
in the Askew Picture
House, **Gateshead**

Few cease to believe
in ghosts, but those
who see them may
still deny they exist-
see **St Leonards**, or
quit their jobs out of
sheer fright.

The Manager , Robert Parrington Jackson, murdered at the Odeon, Bristol in 1946

Ernest Symmons, original owner of the Playhouse, Beverley, who kept a posthumous eye on the cinema

A WORD ABOUT ORBS

Paranormal investigators often report photographing orbs, not always seen beforehand. However, opinion differs as to whether orbs represent the first manifestation of a ghost or spirit, or just a camera malfunction or an atmospheric contamination. A detailed book called *A Beginners guide to Paranormal Investigation* (Amberley, 2013) fairly puts the sceptics case that orbs began to multiply in 1997, simply due to the advent of digital cameras. These can pick up some ultra violet and infrared light, that conventional film cameras and the human eye missed. So either the boundaries between the spirit world and our world are breaking down, or the cameras are picking up floating dust particles. The questions remains why do they appear on night time CCTV when no cleaners are at work or audiences present?

IMPRINTING OR RESIDUAL HAUNTING

Some phenomena are not strictly ghosts as the figures will repeat the same actions to any who witness them, but show no sign of being aware of those present. They may be even walking on a different level. Researchers say this could be just a recording of an event, played back somehow by the building , but the mechanism by which this happens is not yet clear. But we are left with interactive ghosts, who are aware of their witnesses, and whether they are visible - or

Invisible, want our attention. These could be classified as ghosts manifesting evidence for life after death and survival of the soul.

AND WHAT ABOUT COLD SPOTS?

Often reported with or without an apparition. Gordon Smith has an explanation in his book *One hundred answers from Spirit (2016)* He writes: (Spirits) need energy more dense than the Spirit, so from the atmosphere they would use some of the particles to form a denser energy around them, like a cloak. This is why it has been said many times by people who have experienced a vision of a materialised spirit that the air around them turned cold. They felt cold as the particles of heat were drawn together around the forming image.

In 1963 "Summer Holiday" proved a better choice at an Oxford cinema

SOURCES

The Cinema Theatre Association archives, Bulletin and
Picture House; Mercia Bioscope and newsreel, North
West Cinema Preservation Society news;
Websites: Cinematreasures.org; hauntedplaces.org;
mawgrim co uk; paranormaldatabase.com;
www.hauntedhappenings.co.uk; www.ghostbusters.co.uk
and numerous websites for local ghost investigators.

John Benzing; Ben Doman; Harry Rigby, Mike Whitcombe;
Scott Mackinnon and www.phxi.co.uk; Steve Oldfield

ADAMS, Paul and SMITH, Guy N Extreme hauntings:
Britain's most terrifying ghosts (2013); CHARD, Judy
Haunting happenings in Devon (1989) GREEN, Andrew Our
haunted Kingdom (1973); JONES, Richard Walking Haunted
London (2005); LAKIN, Tina Haunted theatres of East
Sussex; ROBINSON, Peter and HESP, P Ghosts of Beverley
and the East Riding (1987); UNDERWOOD, Peter Haunted
London (2010)

STOP PRESS

HULL The ornate Tower cinema, which has had its illegally
removed domes painstakingly replaced, has been a nightclub
since 1983, but in March 2016 the Hull Daily Mail reported
the owner of the Funktion Nightclub has seen some shadowy

figures, doors opening and closing and mysterious footsteps upstairs when the building is empty. Paranormal investigation seemed to confirm all was not normal, but the identity of the spirit(s) is not established, as a death in the actual cinema is not proven.

An early view of the Tower with the original domes (C.T.A)

SWINDON   Ben Doman and colleague were redecorating the ABC. An older woman went up to the usherette's seat, but it was on the other side of the entrance, from where it now was. . The chief later said the seat had been on that side. For an explanation, see remarks for Ramsgate. Ben also worked at the **NEWBURY** ABC , and had experiences there too which are being covered in the Cinema Theatre Association Bulletin.

INDEX

BUCKLEY	70
CARMARTHEN	39, 71
CHATHAM	50, 55
CHESTER	30
CLACTON	7
CLYDEBANK	66
CRAWLEY	55, 58
CREWE	30
DEVIZES	40, 63
DIDSBURY	31
DOVER	56
EAST GRINSTEAD	51
EDINBURGH	67
ELGIN	39, 67
FOLKESTONE	51
GATESHEAD	24, 75
GOSPORT	59, 60
GRAVESEND	52

Euston	36
Nottinghill Gate	37
Peckham	37
Stoke Newington	38, 42
Streatham	33, 38, 47
Worcester Park	47
LONGTON	12
LUTON	7
MANSFIELD	12-13, 43
MIDDLESBROUGH	25, 26
MOTHERWELL	67-69
NEWCASTLE UNDER LYME	13
NORWICH	8
NOTTINGHAM	13-15
OXFORD	14, 43
PAIGNTON	44, 64
PLYMOUTH	64-65
POCKLINGTON	20, 23

OR PERHAPS, SOME OF THE
UNINVITED GUESTS ?

P.S.

There are more ghosts on screen than off it